Religions Around the World

Islam

Anita Ganeri

a Capstone company — publishers for children

Raintree is an imprint of Capstone Global Library Limited, a company incorporated in England and Wales having its registered office at 264 Banbury Road, Oxford, OX2 7DY – Registered company number: 6695582

www.raintree.co.uk
myorders@raintree.co.uk

Edited by Linda Staniford
Designed by Jenny Bergstrom
Picture research by Pam Mitsakos
Production by Steve Walker
Originated by Capstone Global Library
Printed and bound in China

ISBN 978 1 474 74215 3
21 20 19 18 17
10 9 8 7 6 5 4 3 2 1

British Library Cataloguing in Publication Data
A full catalogue record for this book is available from the British Library.

Acknowledgements
We would like to thank the following for permission to reproduce photographs: Getty Images: David Lees, 9, Pacific Press/Prabhat Kumar Verma, 6; iStockphoto: Juanmonino, 24; Newscom: imageBROKER/Olaf Krüger, 20, Pakistan Press International Photo, 10, picture-alliance/CHROMORANGE/Günter Fischer, 8, picture-alliance/Godong/Pascal Deloche, 16, picture-alliance/Godong/Philippe Lissac, 5; Shutterstock: Aleksandar Todorovic, 18, Asianet-Pakistan, 11, AVA Bitter, cover middle, 1 middle, ChameleonsEye, 23, 29, Distinctive Images, 14, JOAT, 27, Kertu, 28, Leila Ablyazova, 12, Luisma Tapia, 17, Mainlake, 15, Mawardi Bahar, 7, mirzavisoko, 25, Moreno Soppelsa, 13, samiph222, design element, shahreen, 4, szefei, 22, Vladimir Melnik, 21, ZouZou, 19, Zurijeta, 26

We would like to thank Reverend Laurence Hillel of the London Inter Faith Centre for his invaluable help in the preparation of this book.

Contents

Some words are shown in bold, **like this.** You can find out what they mean by looking in the glossary.

What is Islam?

Islam is a religion that began in the country we now call Saudi Arabia. It began about 1,400 years ago. Today, more than 1.5 **billion** people follow Islam.

The Ka'bah **shrine** in Makkah, Saudi Arabia, is a very **holy** place for Muslims.

This Muslim family lives in London.

People who follow Islam are called Muslims. Muslims live all over the world. Indonesia is the country with the most Muslims. Around 3 million Muslims live in Britain.

What do Muslims believe?

Muslims believe that there is one God. They call God "Allah". They believe that Allah created the world. They obey Allah's wishes and follow Allah's teaching in their lives.

Saying prayers is very important in Islam.

This **mosque** is in the city of Madinah, Saudi Arabia. Madinah is where the prophet Muhammad died.

Muslims believe that Allah sent messengers to teach people about Islam. These messengers were called **prophets.** The last and greatest prophet was a man named Muhammad.

The Shahadah is written in Arabic over the entrance to **mosques.**

The **Pillars of Islam** are five things that Muslims believe. The first pillar is the Shahadah, the belief that Allah is the only God, and that Muhammad is Allah's **prophet.**

The second pillar is saying prayers (see pages 16–17). Allah told Muslims to pray five times a day. Muslims believe that praying is a way of obeying Allah.

Every day a man called a mu'adhdhin calls people to prayer in the mosque.

The third pillar is giving money to the poor. If they can, Muslims give away some of their money every year. The fourth pillar is **fasting** for the month of **Ramadan** (see pages 26–27).

Muslims give money to the poor at a festival in Lahore, Pakistan.

Muslims wear white to go on the Hajj. Muslims try to visit Makkah at least once in their lives.

The fifth pillar is making Hajj, or a **pilgrimage** to Makkah, in Saudi Arabia. Muhammad was born in Makkah. It is the **holiest** place in the Muslim world.

The Holy Qur'an

The Muslims' **holy** book is called the Qur'an. Muslims believe that the Qur'an is the word of Allah. They treat it with great **respect**. They read it and try to follow its teachings.

Copies of the Qur'an are often beautifully decorated.

Allah's words were later written down in the **Arabic** language. The writings are called the Qur'an.

Muslims believe that Allah gave the words of the Qur'an to Muhammad. Muhammad could not read or write. He learned the words by heart and taught them to his friends.

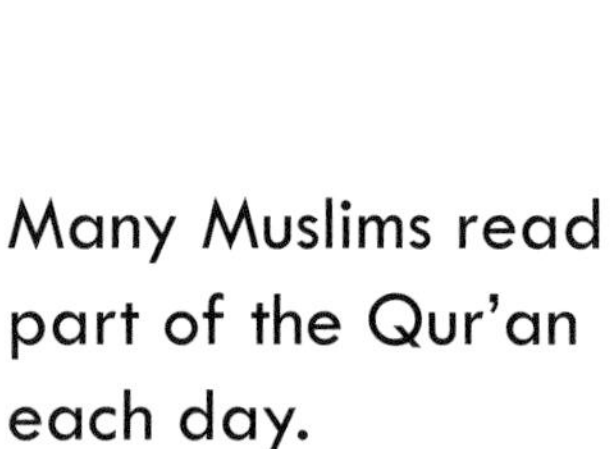

Many Muslims read part of the Qur'an each day.

Some parts of the Qur'an tell Muslims about things that happened in the past. Other parts teach them how to worship Allah and live a good life.

Some Muslims learn the whole of the Qur'an by heart. They do this as a way of praising Allah. They have to keep practising to make sure that they do not forget anything.

These men are learning to recite the Qur'an.

How do Muslims worship?

The Qur’an tells Muslims that they should pray five times a day. The times for prayer are early morning, midday, mid-afternoon, just after sunset and before midnight.

These clocks in a mosque show the times for prayer. One of them shows the time of sunrise, which is the end of the early morning prayer time.

When Muslims pray, they must face towards the **holy** city of Makkah. Every **mosque** has an **arch** in the wall. The arch shows which direction Makkah is.

The arch is called a qiblah. This one is in a mosque in Spain.

Before they pray, Muslims wash in a special way. This helps to make them ready to pray to Allah. They always wash in the same order so that they do not forget anything.

The Qur'an tells Muslims that they must be clean before they pray to Allah.

Muslims can pray on their own, or together in a **mosque**.

As Muslims pray, they follow a **set** pattern of words and actions. They stand up as the prayer begins. Then they bow, kneel and touch the ground with their foreheads.

This mosque is in London. The tower on the right is called a minaret.

Muslims worship in a building called a **mosque.** Muslims go to the mosque to meet and pray. Mosques are also used as schools where young people can learn about Islam.

Fridays are special days for Muslims. All Muslim men try to go to the mosque for midday prayers. A leader, called an imam, gives a talk about Islam. Women can choose if they want to go.

These Muslims have gathered for Friday prayers in a mosque in Iran.

Family life

Family life is very important for Muslims. They love and care for their own families. They must also **respect** all other Muslims, wherever they live in the world.

Muslim children are taught to respect and be kind to their parents.

Muslims must only eat **halal** food, which has been prepared according to Islamic law.

In everyday life, Muslims follow strict rules about food and drink. They are not allowed to eat some kinds of food, such as pork. They are not allowed to drink **alcohol**.

Muslim babies are given a name on the seventh day after they are born.

Muslims believe that children are a gift from Allah. When a baby is born, a prayer is whispered in his or her ear. It asks for the baby to be a good Muslim.

There are three days of official mourning after a Muslim dies.

When a Muslim dies, there is a simple **funeral**. The person is buried, facing towards Makkah. A simple stone marks the grave. **Mourners** say prayers at the graveside.

Fasts and festivals

Every year, Muslims **fast** for the month of **Ramadan.** They do not eat or drink during the day. Fasting is a way of showing that they are living their lives the way Allah wants.

During Ramadan, Muslims are only allowed to eat after the sun goes down.

Muslims give gifts at the Id-ul-Fitr festival.

The end of Ramadan is marked with a festival. It is called Id-ul-Fitr. On Id morning, Muslims go to the **mosque** for prayers. Afterwards, they give each other gifts and cards.

These Muslims are giving packages of food to workers in Dubai.

Id-ul-Adha is another festival. It takes place at the end of the Hajj (see page 11). Muslims share a feast with family and friends. They give some of the food away to the poor.

At Id-ul-Adha, Muslims remember the story of the **Prophet** Ibrahim. He was ready to kill his son, Isma'il, to show his love for Allah, but Allah sent him a sheep to kill instead.

Lamb is traditionally eaten at Id-ul-Adha.

Glossary

alcohol a liquid that can make people drunk, so that they cannot control their actions or emotions

Arabic the religious language of Islam; the Qur'an is written in Arabic

arch curved structure over an opening in a building

billion one thousand million; one followed by nine noughts

fast stop eating food for a given time

funeral ceremony held after someone has died

halal meat that has been prepared according to Islamic law

holy sacred, dedicated to God

mosque building where Muslims worship

mourner person who is very sad and missing someone who has died

pilgrimage long journey to a holy place

Pillars of Islam the five important things that Muslims believe

prophet messenger who teaches people about God

Ramadan month of fasting in the Muslim calendar

respect feeling of admiration or high regard

set fixed, established or provided

shrine place that contains objects associated with a holy person

Find out more

Books

Celebrating Islamic Festivals (Celebration Days), Liz Miles (Raintree, 2015)

Muslim Festivals (A Year of Festivals), Honor Head (Wayland, 2011)

We are Muslims (My Religion and Me), Philip Blake (Franklin Watts, 2015)

Websites

www.bbc.co.uk/schools/religion/islam/
Find out more about Islam with this fact-packed website.

www.primaryhomeworkhelp.co.uk/religion/islam.htm
Lots of information about Islam to help you with homework projects.

Index